SCHOLASTIC

Solve-the-Riddle
Math Practice

50+ Reproducible Activity Sheets That Help Students
Master Key Math Skills—and Solve Rib-Tickling Riddles

LIANE B. ONISH

New York • Toronto • London • Auckland • Sydney
Mexico City • New Delhi • Hong Kong • Buenos Aires

Teaching *Resources*

Hi, Mom!

Cover design by Maria Lilja
Interior design by Holly Grundon
Interior illustrations by Anne Kennedy

ISBN-13: 978-0-545-10102-8
ISBN-10: 0-545-10102-6

Text copyright © 2009 by Liane B. Onish
Illustrations © 2009 by Scholastic Inc.
Published by Scholastic Inc.
Printed in the U.S.A.
3 4 5 6 7 8 9 10   40   16 15 14 13 12 11 10 09

Contents

About This Book

Research shows that to master essential math skills, children need plenty of sustained practice. Quick recall of addition and subtraction facts and understanding of place value and regrouping are essential foundation skills for further success in math. The silly riddles on the activity pages in this book will motivate children to complete the math problems and get this needed practice. Each answer is keyed to a letter. Located below the math problems is the solution to the riddle. Children write the letter that corresponds to each numerical answer to spell out the solution to the riddle. Voila! Math practiced, riddle solved!

Meeting the Math Standards

The National Council of Teachers of Mathematics (NCTM) has outlined learning expectations and focal points—key concepts and skills for emphasis at different grade levels. The activities in this book align with the Numbers and Operations standard and focal points for children in grades 1 and 2 (nctm.org/standards).

For an overview of the specific math skills covered in this book, see the Contents page. (These math skills are also listed at the top of each activity sheet.) Activity pages 5-33 (Riddles 1–29) focus on first grade skills. Pages 34–61 (Riddles 30–57) focus on second grade skills. Use children's different ability levels as a guide when assigning the activity sheets.

Introducing the Activities

Read the riddle and math directions with children. Point out the letter below each answer's write-on line. Explain that the answers have the letters they will use to solve the riddle. After children complete the math, direct them to the bottom of the page. Tell them that they will solve the riddle by using the letters under each answer. Have them read the number under the solution's first blank line. Help children find that number in their math answers. Then have them write the letter that goes with that number answer on the line. When all of the letters have been filled in, invite children to reread the riddle and the solution.

Math Vocabulary Teaching Tip

Review with children math vocabulary used on the activity pages: *add, sum, subtract, difference, ones, tens, regroup.* This is especially helpful for English language learners.

Word Play

The riddles in this book rely mostly on multiple meanings and puns. Use these practice pages for more word play. For example: after completing Riddle 1 "Where do rabbits go after their wedding?" (*on a bunnymoon*), ask children to list words that rhyme with *bunny* (*honey, money, funny*). Then challenge them to make up riddles using these rhyming words and the riddle frame: "Where do _____ go after their wedding?" For example: "Where do clowns go after their wedding?" (*on a funnymoon*)

Riddle 1

Where do rabbits go after their wedding?

Write the missing numbers.
Solve the riddle using your answers below.

1, 2, 3, _____, 5
A

15, 16, 17, _____, 19
O

3, 4, 5, _____, 7
B

17, 18, 19, _____, 21
R

6, 7, 8, _____, 10
C

18, 19, 20, _____, 22
S

8, 9, 10, _____, 12
D

19, 20, 21, _____, 23
T

10, 11, 12, _____, 14
M

20, 21, 22, _____, 24
U

12, 13, 14, _____, 16
N

21, 22, 23, _____, 25
Y

Solve the Riddle! Write the letter that goes with each number.

_____ _____ _____
18   15   4

_____ _____ _____ _____ _____ _____ _____ _____ _____
6   23   15   15   24   13   18   18   15

Name: _____ Date: _____

Riddle 2

Where was the owl
when the lights went out?

Write the missing numbers.
Solve the riddle using your answers below.

28, 29, 30, ____, 32 A	27, 28, 29, ____, 31 D
25, 26, 27 ____, 29 E	26, 27, 28, ____, 30 F
31, 32, 33, ____, 35 H	37, 38, 39, ____, 41 I
33, 34, 35, ____, 37 N	35, 36, 37, ____, 39 K
40, 41, 42, ____, 44 T	38, 39, 40, ____, 42 R
39, 40, 41, ____, 43 S	46, 47, 48, ____, 50 W

Solve the Riddle!   Write the letter that goes with each number.

____ ____   ____ ____ ____
40   36   43   34   28

____ ____ ____ ____
30   31   41   38

Solve-the-Riddle Math Practice © 2009 by Liane B. Onish. Scholastic Teaching Resources

Name: _____   Date: _____

Riddle 3

What kinds of stories does a ship captain read to his kids?

Write the missing numbers.
Solve the riddle using your answers below.

52, 53, 54, _____, 56 A	56, 57, 58 _____, 60 B
53, 54, 55, _____, 57 C	48, 49, 50, _____, 52 F
50, 51, 52, _____, 54 G	57, 58, 59, _____, 61 E
54, 55, 56, _____, 58 I	66, 67, 68, _____, 70 L
68, 69, 70, _____, 72 R	71, 72, 73, _____, 75 S
65, 66, 67, _____, 69 T	69, 70, 71, _____, 73 Y

Solve the Riddle! Write the letter that goes with each number.

_____ _____ _____ _____ _____
51   60   71   71   72

_____ _____ _____ _____ _____
68   55   69   60   74

Name: _____ Date: _____

Riddle 4

Why do lions eat raw meat?

Write the missing numbers.
Solve the riddle using your answers below.

72, 73, 74, _____, 76
A

74, 75, 76, _____, 78
B

78, 79, 80, _____, 82
C

83, 84, 85, _____, 87
D

81, 82, 83, _____, 85
E

76, 77, 78, _____, 80
H

84, 85, 86, _____, 88
K

86, 87, 88, _____, 90
N

88, 89, 90, _____, 92
O

93, 94, 95, _____, 97
T

95, 96, 97, _____, 99
W

96, 97, 98, _____, 100
Y

Solve the Riddle! Write the letter that goes with each number.

,

| 96 | 79 | 84 | 99 | | 86 | 91 | 89 | 96 | | 87 | 89 | 91 | 98 |

| | 79 | 91 | 98 | | 96 | 91 | | 81 | 91 | 91 | 87 | .

Name: _____   Date: _____

Riddle 5

What do you call a monkey who never stops talking?

Write the number for each number word.
Solve the riddle using your answers.

two	_____	nine	_____
	A		O
four	_____	ten	_____
	D		S
zero	_____	three	_____
	N		C
eight	_____	one	_____
	R		L
five	_____	six	_____
	B		P
seven	_____	eleven	_____
	E		Y

Solve the Riddle! Write the letter that goes with each number.

___ ___ ___ ___ ___ - ___ ___ ___
 2   5   I   2   5   9   9   0

Solve-the-Riddle Math Practice © 2009 by Liane B. Onish. Scholastic Teaching Resources

Name: _____   Date: _____

Riddle 6

What do boxers like to drink?

Read the words and write the number.
Solve the riddle using your answers.

one ten and zero ones _____
A

one ten and two ones _____
C

one ten and five ones _____
D

one ten and seven ones _____
E

one ten and four ones _____
H

one ten and nine ones _____
N

one ten and three ones _____
P

two tens and zero ones _____
S

one ten and eight ones _____
W

one ten and one one _____
U

Solve the Riddle!   Write the letter that goes with each number.

_____ _____ _____ _____ _____
  13   11   19   12   14

Solve-the-Riddle Math Practice © 2009 by Liane B. Onish. Scholastic Teaching Resources

Name: _____   Date: _____

Riddle 7

How do you get milk from an elephant?

Circle the larger number.
Solve the riddle using your answers.

$\frac{3}{A}$ or $\frac{2}{B}$	$\frac{17}{W}$ or $\frac{18}{N}$
$\frac{6}{K}$ or $\frac{9}{E}$	$\frac{21}{O}$ or $\frac{20}{S}$
$\frac{11}{F}$ or $\frac{10}{C}$	$\frac{17}{P}$ or $\frac{16}{J}$
$\frac{16}{G}$ or $\frac{6}{L}$	$\frac{4}{M}$ or $\frac{14}{I}$
$\frac{12}{D}$ or $\frac{20}{H}$	$\frac{19}{R}$ or $\frac{9}{S}$
$\frac{13}{F}$ or $\frac{4}{Q}$	$\frac{1}{Z}$ or $\frac{10}{T}$

Solve the Riddle!   Write the letter that goes with each number.

___ ___ ___ ___   ___ ___ ___
21 17 9 18   20 9 19

___ ___ ___ ___ ___ ___ ___ ___ ___ ___ ___ ___.
19 9 13 19 14 16 9 19 3 10 21 19

Name: _____   Date: _____

Riddle 8

What did cave-kids eat for lunch?

Circle the larger number.
Solve the riddle using your answers.

$\dfrac{10}{X}$ or $\dfrac{11}{C}$	$\dfrac{27}{L}$ or $\dfrac{25}{M}$
$\dfrac{12}{Q}$ or $\dfrac{21}{D}$	$\dfrac{15}{P}$ or $\dfrac{51}{N}$
$\dfrac{23}{F}$ or $\dfrac{32}{A}$	$\dfrac{18}{S}$ or $\dfrac{15}{T}$
$\dfrac{41}{E}$ or $\dfrac{14}{G}$	$\dfrac{24}{V}$ or $\dfrac{42}{W}$
$\dfrac{31}{H}$ or $\dfrac{13}{J}$	$\dfrac{39}{R}$ or $\dfrac{49}{U}$
$\dfrac{43}{I}$ or $\dfrac{34}{K}$	$\dfrac{25}{Z}$ or $\dfrac{29}{B}$

Solve the Riddle!   Write the letter that goes with each number.

____ ____ ____ ____
11   27   49   29

____ ____ ____ ____ ____ ____ ____ ____ ____ ____
18   32   51   21   42   43   11   31   41   18

Riddle 9

Name: _____   Date: _____

Riddle 9

Why did Silly Billy wear a baseball mitt?

Circle the larger number.
Solve the riddle using your answers.

$\frac{61}{D}$ or $\frac{16}{F}$	$\frac{96}{R}$ or $\frac{69}{N}$
$\frac{27}{G}$ or $\frac{72}{B}$	$\frac{51}{S}$ or $\frac{15}{P}$
$\frac{83}{C}$ or $\frac{38}{J}$	$\frac{93}{T}$ or $\frac{39}{Q}$
$\frac{74}{E}$ or $\frac{47}{K}$	$\frac{45}{W}$ or $\frac{54}{U}$
$\frac{81}{H}$ or $\frac{18}{L}$	$\frac{49}{V}$ or $\frac{94}{A}$
$\frac{67}{M}$ or $\frac{76}{O}$	$\frac{100}{Z}$ or $\frac{99}{Y}$

Solve the Riddle!   Write the letter that goes with each number.

___ ___   ___ ___ ___ ___ ___
93 76   83 94 93 83 81

___ ___ ___   ___ ___ ___
93 81 74   72 54 51

Name: _____   Date: _____

Riddle 10

What kind of cookies do birds like best?

Add.

Solve the riddle using your answers.

$3 + 5 =$ _____ A	$0 + 3 =$ _____ L
$4 + 2 =$ _____ C	$4 + 6 =$ _____ E
$7 + 2 =$ _____ H	$1 + 0 =$ _____ P
$8 + 3 =$ _____ S	$1 + 1 =$ _____ T
$2 + 2 =$ _____ R	$5 + 2 =$ _____ I
$1 + 4 =$ _____ O	$6 + 6 =$ _____ N

Solve the Riddle! Write the letter that goes with each number.

___ ___ ___ ___ ___ ___ ___ ___ ___
6   9   5   6   5   3   8   2   10

___ ___ ___ ___ ___
6   9   7   4   1

Riddle 11

Name: _____ Date: _____

Where does Santa swim?

Subtract.
Solve the riddle using your answers.

5 – 3 = _____
E

10 – 9 = _____
P

8 – 4 = _____
B

12 – 2 = _____
H

7 – 2 = _____
I

9 – 9 = _____
T

6 – 3 = _____
L

12 – 5 = _____
R

12 – 6 = _____
N

11 – 0 = _____
A

11 – 2 = _____
O

9 – 1 = _____
D

Solve the Riddle! Write the letter that goes with each number.

_____ _____   _____ _____ _____
  5   6   0   10   2

_____ _____ _____ _____ _____   _____ _____ _____ _____
  6   9   7   0   10   1   9   9   3

Name: _____   Date: _____

Riddle 12

What magic words did the mother mouse teach her children?

Add or subtract.

Solve the riddle using your answers.

$6 + 3 =$ _____
A

$11 - 9 =$ _____
O

$12 - 2 =$ _____
C

$4 + 4 =$ _____
H

$8 + 3 =$ _____
D

$12 - 9 =$ _____
S

$10 - 3 =$ _____
E

$4 + 1 =$ _____
T

$5 - 1 =$ _____
K

$12 - 11 =$ _____
U

$10 + 2 =$ _____
N

$1 + 5 =$ _____
Y

Solve the Riddle!   Write the letter that goes with each number.

___ ___ ___ ___ ___ ___   ___ ___ ___
10   8   7   7   3   7   9   12   11

___ ___ ___ ___ ___   ___ ___ ___
5   8   9   12   4   6   2   1

Name: _____ Date: _____

Riddle 13

Why did the circus tiger spit out the clown?

Add or subtract.
Solve the riddle using your answers.

$4 + 8 = $ _____
A

$5 + 6 = $ _____
P

$12 - 8 = $ _____
E

$11 - 5 = $ _____
Y

$12 - 4 = $ _____
D

$11 - 6 = $ _____
U

$10 - 3 = $ _____
H

$2 + 7 = $ _____
S

$10 - 7 = $ _____
N

$9 - 7 = $ _____
T

$3 + 7 = $ _____
F

$7 + 2 = $ _____
S

Solve the Riddle! Write the letter that goes with each number.

___ ___   ___ ___ ___ ___ ___ ___
7   4   2   12 9   2   4   8

___ ___ ___ ___ ___ .
10 5   3   3   6

Riddle  14

What kind of witch lives on the beach?

Add.

Solve the riddle using your answers.

$16 + 8 =$ _____
N

$8 + 2 =$ _____
I

$12 + 4 =$ _____
S

$13 + 2 =$ _____
J

$14 + 4 =$ _____
H

$10 + 1 =$ _____
F

$9 + 3 =$ _____
T

$6 + 8 =$ _____
R

$7 + 6 =$ _____
A

$9 + 8 =$ _____
D

$20 + 5 =$ _____
W

$13 + 6 =$ _____
C

Solve the Riddle!   Write the letter that goes with each number.

____ ____ ____ ____ ____ -
13   16   13   24   17

____ ____ ____ ____ ____
25   10   12   19   18

Name: _____ Date: _____

Riddle 15

Where do books sleep?

Subtract.
Solve the riddle using your answers.

$25 - 7 =$ _____
E

$22 - 11 =$ _____
S

$19 - 4 =$ _____
O

$24 - 5 =$ _____
R

$14 - 4 =$ _____
T

$25 - 3 =$ _____
C

$16 - 7 =$ _____
V

$16 - 8 =$ _____
U

$23 - 6 =$ _____
N

$21 - 5 =$ _____
D

$18 - 5 =$ _____
D

$13 - 6 =$ _____
H

Solve the Riddle! Write the letter that goes with each number.

___ ___ ___ ___ ___   ___ ___ ___
8   17   13   18   19   10   7   18

___ ___ ___ ___ ___ ___
22   15   9   18   19   11

Name: _____ Date: _____

Riddle 16

Why didn't the sad frog jump?

Add or subtract.
Solve the riddle using your answers.

21 – 5 = ____ A	20 – 9 = ____ Y
18 + 4 = ____ H	13 + 6 = ____ S
24 – 6 = ____ E	14 – 8 = ____ W
16 + 7 = ____ N	17 + 3 = ____ U
23 + 2 = ____ O	15 + 9 = ____ P
19 – 5 = ____ T	25 – 16 = ____ R

Solve the Riddle! Write the letter that goes with each number.

____ ____   ____ ____ ____   ____ ____ ____
22   18   6   16   19   14   25   25

____ ____ ____ ____ ____ ____ ____ .
20   23   22   25   24   24   11

Name: _____ Date: _____

Riddle 17

What do you get when you cross a stream and a river?

Add.

Solve the riddle using your answers.

10 + 50 = _____ A	50 + 10 = _____ A
10 + 40 = _____ B	70 + 10 = _____ T
20 + 10 = _____ E	10 + 0 = _____ N
30 + 10 = _____ K	60 + 10 = _____ W
10 + 10 = _____ R	90 + 10 = _____ D
80 + 10 = _____ S	10 + 80 = _____ S

Solve the Riddle! Write the letter that goes with each number.

_____ _____ _____
70   30   80

_____ _____ _____ _____ _____ _____ _____ _____
90   10   30   60   40   30   20   90

Solve-the-Riddle Math Practice © 2009 by Liane B. Onish. Scholastic Teaching Resources

Name: _____   Date: _____

Riddle 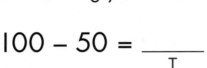 18

How is a pig in the house like a house on fire?

Subtract.
Solve the riddle using your answers.

100 – 50 = _____ T	50 – 50 = _____ I
70 – 40 = _____ U	100 – 20 = _____ B
30 – 20 = _____ O	80 – 10 = _____ E
50 – 30 = _____ H	60 – 20 = _____ S
70 – 10 = _____ R	100 – 0 = _____ L
100 – 10 = _____ N	70 – 20 = _____ T

Solve the Riddle! Write the letter that goes with each number.

$\overline{}$ $\overline{}$ $\overline{}$ $\overline{}$ $\overline{}$ $\overline{}$ $\overline{}$ $\overline{}$ $\overline{}$ $\overline{}$ $\overline{}$ $\overline{}$ $\overline{}$
50 20 70   40 10 10 90 70 60   0 50   0 40

$\overline{}$ $\overline{}$ $\overline{}$, $\overline{}$ $\overline{}$ $\overline{}$ $\overline{}$ $\overline{}$ $\overline{}$ $\overline{}$ $\overline{}$ $\overline{}$!
10 30 50   50 20 70   80 70 50 50 70 60

Name: _____   Date: _____

Riddle 19

When is the best time to eat lunch?

Add or subtract.
Solve the riddle using your answers.

90 − 50 = _____ F	50 + 50 = _____ T
40 + 40 = _____ L	100 − 20 = _____ L
70 − 50 = _____ O	80 + 10 = _____ S
80 − 80 = _____ E	60 + 0 = _____ B
60 − 10 = _____ A	90 − 80 = _____ R
100 − 30 = _____ K	10 + 20 = _____ D

Solve the Riddle!   Write the letter that goes with each number.

_____ _____ _____ _____ _____
50   40   100   0   10

_____ _____ _____ _____ _____ _____ _____ _____ _____
60   10   0   50   70   40   50   90   100

Name: _____ Date: _____

Riddle 20

Why did the horse need a doctor?

Count by 2's. Write the missing numbers.
Solve the riddle using your answers.

2, 4, 6, _____
A

30, 32, 34, _____
S

4, 6, 8, _____
D

36, 38, 40, _____
O

10, 12, 14, _____
E

34, 36, 38, _____
T

14, 16, 18, _____
F

40, 42, 44, _____
Y

22, 24, 26, _____
H

42, 44, 46, _____
W

26, 28, 30, _____
R

44, 46, 48, _____
V

Solve the Riddle! Write the letter that goes with each number.

_____ _____   _____ _____ _____
28   16   28   8   10

_____ _____ _____   _____ _____ _____ _____ _____.
28   8   46   20   16   50   16   32

Name: _____   Date: _____

Riddle 21

What do little dogs eat at the movies?

Count down by 2's. Write the missing numbers.
Solve the riddle using your answers.

40, 38, 36, _____
B

22, 20, 18, _____
O

46, 44, 42, _____
D

38, 36, 34, _____
A

30, 28, 26, _____
P

24, 22, 20, _____
T

50, 48, 46, _____
N

12, 10, 8, _____
E

28, 26, 24, _____
U

26, 24, 22, _____
C

34, 32, 30, _____
R

16, 14, 12, _____
S

Solve the Riddle!   Write the letter that goes with each number.

___ ___ ___ ___ ___ ___ ___ ___
34 22 18 18   6   28   6   40

___ ___ ___ - ___ ___ ___ ___
24 22 24   20 16 28 44

Riddle 22

Name: _____ Date: _____

How many apples grow on a tree?

Add or subtract.
Solve the riddle using your answers.

40 + 2 = _____
O

10 – 2 = _____
T

20 – 2 = _____
F

30 + 2 = _____
R

50 – 2 = _____
S

10 + 2 = _____
L

10 + 2 = _____
D

40 – 2 = _____
M

30 – 2 = _____
A

48 + 2 = _____
H

20 + 2 = _____
E

2 + 2 = _____
N

Solve the Riddle! Write the letter that goes with each number.

_____ _____ _____   _____ _____
28   12   12   42   18

_____ _____ _____ _____
8   50   22   38

Name: _____   Date: _____

Riddle 23

Which side of a house gets the most rain?

Count by 5's. Write the missing numbers.
Solve the riddle using your answers.

10, 15, 20, _____ E	45, 50, 60, _____ I
30, 35, 40, _____ N	15, 20, 25, _____ S
40, 45, 50, _____ T	25, 30, 35, _____ F
60, 65, 70, _____ R	35, 40, 45, _____ U
80, 85, 90, _____ O	85, 90, 95, _____ D
55, 60, 65, _____ H	75, 80, 85, _____ B

Solve the Riddle!   Write the letter that goes with each number.

_____ _____ _____
55   70   25

_____ _____ _____ _____ _____ _____ _____
95   50   55   30   65   100   25

Name: _____   Date: _____

Riddle 24

What do friendly cats say to each other?

Count down by 5's. Write the missing numbers.
Solve the riddle using your answers.

20, 15, 10, _____ A	55, 50, 45, _____ V
40, 35, 30, _____ Y	25, 20, 15, _____ N
50, 45, 40, _____ E	35, 30, 25, _____ H
70, 65, 60, _____ C	45, 40, 35, _____ E
90, 85, 80, _____ M	100, 95, 90, _____ T
75, 70, 65, _____ D	65, 60, 55, _____ I

Solve the Riddle!   Write the letter that goes with each number.

____ ____ ____ ____ ____
20   5   40   30   5

____ ____ ____ ____   ____ ____ ____ .
75   50   55   35   60   5   25

Riddle 25

Name: _____   Date: _____

What do naughty little wolves turn into?

Add or subtract.
Solve the riddle using your answers.

$30 + 5 =$ _____
G

$10 - 5 =$ _____
L

$25 - 5 =$ _____
W

$80 - 5 =$ _____
A

$35 + 5 =$ _____
N

$10 + 5 =$ _____
S

$85 + 5 =$ _____
D

$50 - 5 =$ _____
I

$30 - 5 =$ _____
B

$25 + 5 =$ _____
V

$95 + 5 =$ _____
O

$100 - 5 =$ _____
E

Solve the Riddle!   Write the letter that goes with each number.

___ ___ ___   ___ ___ ___
25   45   35   25   75   90

___ ___ ___ ___ ___ ___
20 100   5   30   95   15

Name: _____ Date: _____

Riddle 26

What does the ocean do when it sees the beach?

Circle the two numbers that make 10. Then add.
Solve the riddle using your answers.

Example:

$(5) + (5) + 10 = 20$

$3 + 7 + 4 =$ ____
                 W

$5 + 1 + 5 =$ ____
                 R

$6 + 4 + 9 =$ ____
                 V

$8 + 2 + 10 =$ ____
                  A

$5 + 3 + 7 =$ ____
                 I

$3 + 6 + 4 =$ ____
                 S

$2 + 7 + 8 =$ ____
                 E

$6 + 2 + 4 =$ ____
                 N

$5 + 8 + 5 =$ ____
                 T

Solve the Riddle!   Write the letter that goes with each number.

____ ____   ____ ____ ____ ____ ____ .
 15   18   14   20   19   17   13

Solve-the-Riddle Math Practice © 2009 by Liane B. Onish. Scholastic Teaching Resources

Riddle 27

Name: _____ Date: _____

What did one pig say to the other?

Circle the two numbers that make 10. Then add.
Solve the riddle using your answers.

Example:

$35 + ⑦ + ③ = 45$

$25 + 3 + 7 =$ _____
E

$4 + 6 + 40 =$ _____
T

$35 + 6 + 4 =$ _____
R

$30 + 5 + 5 =$ _____
A

$1 + 5 + 9 =$ _____
S

$20 + 7 + 3 =$ _____
L

$6 + 0 + 4 =$ _____
N

$8 + 2 + 10 =$ _____
P

$5 + 15 + 5 =$ _____
B

Solve the Riddle! Write the letter that goes with each number.

_____ _____ _____ _____   _____ _____
30   35   50   15   25   35

_____ _____ _____   _____ _____ _____ _____ .
20   35   10   20   40   30   15

Name: _____   Date: _____

Riddle 28

Why did Charlie Chicken cross the playground?

Add or subtract.
Solve the riddle using your answers.

$6 + 6 =$ _____
A

$60 + 10 =$ _____
L

$11 - 2 =$ _____
D

$70 - 20 =$ _____
O

_____ $+ 3 = 10$
E

$85 - 5 =$ _____
T

$10 -$ _____ $= 2$
G

$40 - 2 =$ _____
N

$18 - 5 =$ _____
H

$7 + 2 + 8 =$ _____
S

$15 + 9 =$ _____
I

$4 + 5 + 6 =$ _____
R

Solve the Riddle! Write the letter that goes with each number.

___ ___   ___ ___ ___   ___ ___   ___ ___ ___
80 50   8   7   80   80 50   80 13 7

___ ___ ___ ___ ___   ___ ___ ___ ___ ___
50 80 13 7   15   17 70 24 9   7

Name: _____ Date: _____

Riddle 29

What's the difference between a bat and a fly?

Add or subtract.
Solve the riddle using your answers.

$$4 + 5 = \underline{\hspace{1cm}}$$
B

$$50 + 10 = \underline{\hspace{1cm}}$$
Y

$$8 - 3 = \underline{\hspace{1cm}}$$
F

$$80 - 30 = \underline{\hspace{1cm}}$$
N

$$\underline{\hspace{1cm}} + 4 = 10$$
T

$$95 - 5 = = \underline{\hspace{1cm}}$$
R

$$\underline{\hspace{1cm}} - 2 = 10$$
C

$$50 - 2 = \underline{\hspace{1cm}}$$
U

$$17 - 3 = \underline{\hspace{1cm}}$$
L

$$3 + 7 + 7 = \underline{\hspace{1cm}}$$
E

$$14 + 6 = \underline{\hspace{1cm}}$$
A

$$4 + 5 + 6 = \underline{\hspace{1cm}}$$
O

Solve the Riddle!   Write the letter that goes with each number.

$\overline{\hspace{0.5cm}}$ $\overline{\hspace{0.5cm}}$ $\overline{\hspace{0.5cm}}$ $\overline{\hspace{0.5cm}}$ $\overline{\hspace{0.5cm}}$ $\overline{\hspace{0.5cm}}$ $\overline{\hspace{0.5cm}}$ $\overline{\hspace{0.5cm}}$ $\overline{\hspace{0.5cm}}$ $\overline{\hspace{0.5cm}}$ $\overline{\hspace{0.5cm}}$ $\overline{\hspace{0.5cm}}$ $\overline{\hspace{0.5cm}}$
20   9 20 6   12 20 50   5 14 60   9 48 6

$\overline{\hspace{0.5cm}}$ $\overline{\hspace{0.5cm}}$ $\overline{\hspace{0.5cm}}$ $\overline{\hspace{0.5cm}}$ $\overline{\hspace{0.5cm}}$ $\overline{\hspace{0.5cm}}$ $\overline{\hspace{0.5cm}}$ $\overline{\hspace{0.5cm}}$ $\overline{\hspace{0.5cm}}$ $\overline{\hspace{0.5cm}}$ $\overline{\hspace{0.5cm}}$.
20   5 14 60   12 20 50 6   9 20 6

Solve-the-Riddle Math Practice © 2009 by Liane B. Onish. Scholastic Teaching Resources

Name: _____ Date: _____

Riddle (30)

What is black and white and lives in Hawaii?

Write the missing numbers.
Solve the riddle using your answers.

124, _____, 126
   B

316, _____, 318
   T

187, _____, 189
   E

425, _____, 427
   U

149, _____, 151
   N

443, _____, 445
   G

276, _____, 278
   L

251, _____, 253
   I

288, _____, 290
   O

489, _____, 491
   S

301, _____, 303
   S

406, _____, 408
   P

Solve the Riddle! Write the letter that goes with each number.

____ ____ ____   ____ ____ ____ ____
289   150   188   277   289   302   317

____ ____ ____ ____ ____ ____ ____
407   188   150   444   426   252   150

Name: _____   Date: _____

Riddle 31

Which dinosaur always finishes in third place?

Write the missing numbers.
Solve the riddle using your answers.

501, _____, 503	859, _____, 861
B	S
699, _____, 701	925, _____, 927
Z	D
549, _____, 551	744, _____, 746
U	O
687, _____, 689	825, _____, 827
M	N
828, _____, 830	989, _____, 991
R	A
717, _____, 719	906, _____, 908
E	T

Solve the Riddle!   Write the letter that goes with each number.

___ ___ ___ ___ ___ ___ -
502   829   745   826   700   718

___ ___ ___ ___ ___ ___ ___
990   860   990   550   829   550   860

Name: _____ Date: _____

Riddle 32

What is a sea monster's favorite snack?

Read the words and write the number.
Solve the riddle using your answers.

three tens and six ones _____ T	four tens and eight ones _____ H
two tens and five ones _____ E	one ten and nine ones _____ U
eight tens and one one _____ N	five tens and three ones _____ A
six tens and zero ones _____ S	two tens and nine ones _____ I
seven tens and seven ones _____ O	one ten and two ones _____ P

Solve the Riddle! Write the letter that goes with each number.

_____ _____ _____ _____ _____ _____
12   77   36   53   36   77

_____ _____ _____ _____ _____
60   48   29   12   60

Solve-the-Riddle Math Practice © 2009 by Liane B. Onish. Scholastic Teaching Resources

Riddle 33

Name: _____   Date: _____

What animals never tell the truth?

Read the words and write the number.
Solve the riddle using your answers.

two tens and ten ones _____ F	five tens and thirteen ones _____ I
four tens and sixteen ones _____ S	five tens and sixteen ones _____ M
two tens and fifteen ones _____ E	two tens and twenty ones _____ B
one ten and eighteen ones _____ R	seven tens and seventeen ones _____ A
eight tens and eleven ones _____ N	six tens and twelve ones _____ P

Solve the Riddle!   Write the letter that goes with each number.

___ ___ - ___ ___ ___ - ___ ___ ___ ___
87   66   30   63   40   63   87   91   56

Name: _____   Date: _____

Riddle 34

What runs but never walks?

Read the words and write the number.
Solve the riddle using your answers.

one hundred, two tens, five ones _____ A	nine hundreds, two tens, two ones _____ C
two hundreds, zero tens, six ones _____ E	three hundreds, nine tens, zero ones _____ N
six hundreds, three tens, four ones _____ W	four hundreds, one ten, one one _____ D
five hundreds, one ten, nine ones _____ T	eight hundreds, one ten, seven ones _____ R

Solve the Riddle!   Write the letter that goes with each number.

____ ____ ____ ____ ____
634   125   519   206   817

Name: _____   Date: _____

Riddle 35

When are lumberjacks busiest?

Count by 3's. Write the missing numbers.
Solve the riddle using your answers.

0, 3, ____, 9 B	____, 66, 69, 72 O
9, 12, ____, 18 D	____, 78, 81, 84 V
18, 21, ____, 27 R	84, ____, 90, 93 U
27, 30, ____, 36 E	93, ____, 99, 102 I
____, 42, 45, 48 T	105, ____, 111, 114 S
____, 54, 57, 60 M	117, ____, 123, 127 P

Solve the Riddle!   Write the letter that goes with each number.

__ __ __ - __ __ __ __ __ __ __ __!
108 33 120   39   96   51   51   51   6   33   24

Name: _____   Date: _____

Riddle 36

What has a foot on each side and one in the middle?

Count by 4's. Write the missing numbers.
Solve the riddle using your answers.

0, 4, ____, 12
    A

16, 20, ____, 28
      N

32, 36, ____, 44
      D

48, 52, ____, 60
      C

____, 68, 72, 76
 K

____, 84, 88, 92
 R

____, 100, 104, 108
 O

____, 116, 120, 124
 S

128, ____, 136, 140
     I

144, ____, 152, 156
     Y

160, ____, 168, 172
     T

176, ____, 184, 188
     M

Solve the Riddle!   Write the letter that goes with each number.

____
 8

____   ____   ____   ____   ____   ____   ____   ____   ____
148   8   80   40   112   164   132   56   64

Name: _____   Date: _____

Riddle 37

What do you call a hippopotamus with measles?

Count by 5's. Write the missing numbers.
Solve the riddle using your answers.

| 0, 5, _____ | _____, 90, 95 |
| S | A |

| 15, 20, _____ | _____, 105, 110 |
| I | E |

| 30, 35, _____ | 115, _____, 125 |
| Y | P |

| 45, 50, _____ | 130, _____, 140 |
| O | T |

| _____, 65, 70 | 145, _____, 155 |
| U | M |

| _____, 75, 80 | 160, _____, 170 |
| R | H |

Solve the Riddle!   Write the letter that goes with each number.

_____ _____ _____ _____ _____ _____ -
85   165   25   120   120   55

_____ _____ _____ _____ _____ _____ - _____ _____ _____
10   120   55   135   135   40   150   60   10

Name: _____ Date: _____

Riddle 38

What flowers grow right under your nose?

Count by 2's, 3's, and 5's.
Write the missing numbers.
Solve the riddle using your answers.

(+2)	100, _____, E 104	106, _____, T 110	112, _____, A 116	118, _____, I 122
(+3)	120, 123, _____ S	129, 132, _____ N	138, 141, _____ U	147, 150, _____ R
(+5)	175, _____, L 185	190, _____, D 200	205, _____, F 215	220, _____, P 230

Solve the Riddle! Write the letter that goes with each number.

___ ___ ___ ___ ___ ___
108 144 180 120 225 126

Name: _____   Date: _____

Riddle 39

What kind of house weighs the least?

Count by 3's, 4's and 5's.
Write the missing numbers.
Solve the riddle using your answers.

+3	156, 159, ___ T	165, 168, ___ U	174, 177, ___ E	183, 186, ___ L
+4	192, 196, ___ H	204, 208, ___ A	216, 220, ___ G	228, 232, ___ R
+5	235, ___ N 245	250, ___ O 260	265, ___ I 275	285, ___ S 295

Solve the Riddle!   Write the letter that goes with each number.

___
212

___ ___ ___ ___ ___ ___ ___ ___ ___ ___
189 270 224 200 162 200 255 171 290 180

Riddle 40

Name: _____   Date: _____

What did the big grape say to the little grape in December?

Add.

Solve the riddle using your answers.

13	23	10	42	10	11
+15	+11	+ 6	+ 7	+25	+16
S	H	O	A	T	N

44	34	15	36	32	12
+ 4	+12	+11	+ 2	+10	+11
B	J	Y	I	E	L

Solve the Riddle!   Write the letter that goes with each number.

'___ ___ ___   ___ ___ ___   ___ ___ ___ ___ ___ ___
35   38   28   35   34   42   28   42   49   28   16   27

___ ___   ___ ___   ___ ___ ___ ___ ___ !
35   16   48   42   46   42   23   23   26

Solve-the-Riddle Math Practice © 2009 by Liane B. Onish. Scholastic Teaching Resources

Riddle 41

Name: _____   Date: _____

Where can you find health, wealth, and happiness?

Add.
Solve the riddle using your answers.

51	24	30	47	45	72
+12	+62	+61	+32	+21	+26
T	D	R	A	E	I

54	83	51	36	42	28
+21	+11	+21	+21	+40	+60
O	Y	N	H	C	F

Solve the Riddle!   Write the letter that goes with each number.

___ ___   ___
98 72   79

___ ___ ___ ___ ___ ___ ___ ___ ___
86 98 82 63 98 75 72 79 91 94

Name: _____   Date: _____

Riddle 42

How does a witch tell time?

Add.
Solve the riddle using your answers.

54	27	43	38	15	42
+12	+62	+35	+11	+21	+26
___	___	___	___	___	___
S	A	K	O	L	H

31	62	10	42	42	35
+16	+23	+32	+12	+50	+63
___	___	___	___	___	___
W	R	C	E	T	I

Solve the Riddle!   Write the letter that goes with each number.

___ ___ ___   ___ ___ ___ ___ ___   ___ ___   ___ ___ ___
66 68 54   36 49 49 78 66   89 92   68 54 85

___ ___ ___ ___ ___   ___ ___ ___ ___ ___ .
47 98 92 42 68   47 89 92 42 68

Name: _____ Date: _____

What can you do better than anyone else?

Add.
Solve the riddle using your answers.

49	63	39	47	45	46
−12	−30	−21	−42	−21	−16
___	___	___	___	___	___
Y	B	O	F	N	L

- -

48	33	55	36	42	38
− 5	−22	−41	−11	−40	−10
___	___	___	___	___	___
D	U	T	E	R	S

Solve the Riddle! Write the letter that goes with each number.

___ ___
33 25

___ ___ ___ ___ ___ ___ ___ ___.
37 18 11 2 28 25 30 5

Name: _____   Date: _____

Riddle 44

What kind of dinosaur is always ready for bed?

Subtract.

Solve the riddle using your answers.

74	86	93	57	64	99
−51	−42	−12	−22	−22	−36
——	——	——	——	——	——
J	T	A	R	W	M

54	83	98	63	92	83
−22	−22	−14	−13	−22	−10
——	——	——	——	——	——
E	N	P	X	S	U

Solve the Riddle!   Write the letter that goes with each number.

___ ___ ___ ___ ___ ___ ___ -
81   84   81   23   81   63   81

___ ___ ___ ___ ___ ___   ___ ___ ___
70   81   73   35   73   70   35   32   50

---

48   Solve-the-Riddle Math Practice © 2009 by Liane B. Onish. Scholastic Teaching Resources

Name: _____   Date: _____

What do you call cows working together?

Add or subtract.
Solve the riddle using your answers below.

12 +35	59 −23	12 +14	87 −56	27 +11	39 −25
A	C	D	E	G	T

21 +24	64 −51	11 +14	65 −33	11 +26	86 −42
I	N	O	P	R	W

Solve the Riddle!   Write the letter that goes with each number.

___ ___ ___ -
36   25   44

___ ___ ___ ___ ___ ___ ___ ___
25   32   31   37   47   14   45   25   13

Riddle 46

Name: _____ Date: _____

What do you get if you cross an ape and a flower?

Add or subtract.

33 +23	29 −12	61 +31	79 −61	24 +22	89 −80
___ A	___ P	___ T	___ S	___ C	___ G

40 +43	37 −14	53 +21	79 −51	31 +20	99 −50
___ H	___ I	___ K	___ M	___ N	___ Y

Solve the Riddle!   Write the letter that goes with each number.

_____
56

___ ___ ___ ___ - ___ ___ ___ ___ ___
46   83   23   28   17   56   51   18   49

Solve-the-Riddle Math Practice © 2009 by Liane B. Onish. Scholastic Teaching Resources

Riddle 47

Name: _____   Date: _____

Why do bananas use suntan lotion?

Regroup to add.
Solve the riddle using your answers.

$$\begin{array}{r} 12 \\ + 9 \\ \hline \end{array}$$
E

$$\begin{array}{r} 14 \\ + 8 \\ \hline \end{array}$$
P

$$\begin{array}{r} 13 \\ + 7 \\ \hline \end{array}$$
A

$$\begin{array}{r} 18 \\ + 9 \\ \hline \end{array}$$
L

$$\begin{array}{r} 16 \\ + 9 \\ \hline \end{array}$$
B

$$\begin{array}{r} 15 \\ + 9 \\ \hline \end{array}$$
N

$$\begin{array}{r} 19 \\ +11 \\ \hline \end{array}$$
T

$$\begin{array}{r} 14 \\ + 9 \\ \hline \end{array}$$
U

$$\begin{array}{r} 19 \\ + 9 \\ \hline \end{array}$$
S

$$\begin{array}{r} 18 \\ + 8 \\ \hline \end{array}$$
C

$$\begin{array}{r} 14 \\ +16 \\ \hline \end{array}$$
D

$$\begin{array}{r} 11 \\ + 9 \\ \hline \end{array}$$
A

Solve the Riddle!   Write the letter that goes with each number.

___ ___ ___ ___ ___ ___ ___
25 21 26 20 23 28 21

___ ___ ___ ___ ___ ___ ___   ___ ___ ___ ___
25 20 24 20 24 20 28   22 21 21 27

Riddle 48

Name: _____   Date: _____

What dessert do kittens like best?

Regroup to add.
Solve the riddle using your answers.

$$
\begin{array}{r} 23 \\ + 9 \\ \hline \end{array}
\qquad
\begin{array}{r} 38 \\ + 8 \\ \hline \end{array}
\qquad
\begin{array}{r} 26 \\ + 9 \\ \hline \end{array}
\qquad
\begin{array}{r} 18 \\ +24 \\ \hline \end{array}
\qquad
\begin{array}{r} 18 \\ +29 \\ \hline \end{array}
\qquad
\begin{array}{r} 15 \\ +16 \\ \hline \end{array}
$$

I   R   D   E   O   B

$$
\begin{array}{r} 27 \\ +17 \\ \hline \end{array}
\qquad
\begin{array}{r} 28 \\ +12 \\ \hline \end{array}
\qquad
\begin{array}{r} 19 \\ +18 \\ \hline \end{array}
\qquad
\begin{array}{r} 38 \\ + 7 \\ \hline \end{array}
\qquad
\begin{array}{r} 25 \\ +25 \\ \hline \end{array}
\qquad
\begin{array}{r} 19 \\ +29 \\ \hline \end{array}
$$

M   A   C   S   F   N

Solve the Riddle!   Write the letter that goes with each number.

___ ___ ___ ___   ___ ___ ___ ___ ___
44 32 37 42   37 46 42 40 44

___ ___ ___ ___ ___
37 47 48 42 45

Riddle 49

Name: _____   Date: _____

What does an artist do on her day off?

Regroup to add.
Solve the riddle using your answers.

25	38	66	28	26	52
+48	+28	+19	+34	+29	+39
___	___	___	___	___	___
A	S	I	R	K	P

- -

29	38	39	53	22	39
+47	+19	+49	+17	+39	+59
___	___	___	___	___	___
W	T	L	H	E	N

Solve the Riddle!   Write the letter that goes with each number.

___ ___ ___   ___ ___ ___ ___ ___
66   70   61   57   73   55   61   66

___ ___   ___ ___ ___ ___ ___ .
85   57   61   73   66   61   88

Name: _____ Date: _____

Riddle 50

Why didn't Silly Sally use toothpaste?

Regroup to subtract.
Solve the riddle using your answers.

22	24	23	28	26	23
− 9	− 8	−17	−19	− 8	−16
___	___	___	___	___	___
R	E	L	W	N	T

30	24	26	22	21	30
− 5	− 9	− 9	− 8	−18	−11
___	___	___	___	___	___
P	D	S	Y	O	H

Solve the Riddle! Write the letter that goes with each number.

___ ___ ___ ___ ___ ___ ___ ___
19 16 13   7 16 16   7   19

___ ___ ___ ___ ___ ___ ___ ___ ___ ___ ___ ___ .
9 16 13 16 18   3   7   6   3   3 17 16

Solve-the-Riddle Math Practice © 2009 by Liane B. Onish. Scholastic Teaching Resources

Name: _____   Date: _____

Riddle 51

How did the band march in the parade?

Regroup to subtract.
Solve the riddle using your answers.

45	23	47	34	50	31
−28	−17	−29	−19	−29	−12
___	___	___	___	___	___
B	N	S	U	M	T

42	50	20	45	32	50
−19	−43	−11	−17	−16	−24
___	___	___	___	___	___
E	A	D	W	O	H

Solve the Riddle!   Write the letter that goes with each number.

___ ___ ___ ___   ___ ___ ___
19   15   17   7   19   28   16

Solve-the-Riddle Math Practice © 2009 by Liane B. Onish. Scholastic Teaching Resources

Name: _____ Date: _____

Riddle 52

What has four legs and says, "oom-oom"?

Regroup to subtract.
Solve the riddle using your answers.

42	98	47	94	90	61
−28	−19	−29	−19	−29	−23
W	R	A	N	S	C

52	70	70	65	82	92
−19	−43	−21	−36	−24	−25
I	K	G	D	B	O

Solve the Riddle! Write the letter that goes with each number.

___ ___ ___ ___   ___ ___ ___ ___ ___
18   38   67   14   49   67   33   75   49

   ___ ___ ___ ___ ___ ___ ___ ___
    58   18   38   27   14   18   79   29   61

Name: _____   Date: _____

Riddle 53

What did the mommy firefly say to her babies at night?

Regroup to add or subtract.
Solve the riddle using your answers.

22	19	25	18	16	24
− 8	+ 6	−16	+ 6	+ 6	− 7
____	____	____	____	____	____
G	R	L	N	O	T

18	54	21	17	23	12
+ 5	−19	− 9	+ 3	−16	+ 9
____	____	____	____	____	____
P	I	S	A	W	E

Solve the Riddle!   Write the letter that goes with each number.

___ ___ ___   ___ ___ ___ ___
24 22   7   14   9   22   7

___ ___   ___ ___ ___ ___ ___.
17 22   12   9   21 21 23

Name: _____   Date: _____

Riddle 54

Why are elephants so full of wrinkles?

Regroup to add or subtract.
Solve the riddle using your answers.

$$\begin{array}{r} 35 \\ -27 \\ \hline \end{array}$$
E

$$\begin{array}{r} 44 \\ -16 \\ \hline \end{array}$$
O

$$\begin{array}{r} 27 \\ -\ 8 \\ \hline \end{array}$$
B

$$\begin{array}{r} 24 \\ -15 \\ \hline \end{array}$$
Y

$$\begin{array}{r} 40 \\ -19 \\ \hline \end{array}$$
G

$$\begin{array}{r} 21 \\ -16 \\ \hline \end{array}$$
T

$$\begin{array}{r} 32 \\ -14 \\ \hline \end{array}$$
A

$$\begin{array}{r} 40 \\ -23 \\ \hline \end{array}$$
S

$$\begin{array}{r} 23 \\ -16 \\ \hline \end{array}$$
H

$$\begin{array}{r} 50 \\ -11 \\ \hline \end{array}$$
I

$$\begin{array}{r} 33 \\ -18 \\ \hline \end{array}$$
N

$$\begin{array}{r} 41 \\ -27 \\ \hline \end{array}$$
R

Solve the Riddle! Write the letter that goes with each number.

___ ___ ___ ___   ___ ___ ___   ___ ___ ___
5   7   8   9   18 14   8   5 28 28

___ ___ ___   ___ ___   ___ ___ ___ ___ .
19 39 21   5   28   39 14 28 15

Name: _____   Date: _____

Riddle 55

Where does a rabbit go to get her eyes checked?

Add or subtract.
Solve the riddle using your answers.

46	88	72	97	80	68
+13	−27	+24	−35	−27	+24
——	——	——	——	——	——
R	O	H	I	E	A

72	57	49	99	43	93
−17	+23	+26	−17	+29	−50
——	——	——	——	——	——
M	D	S	P	N	T

Solve the Riddle!   Write the letter that goes with each number.

___ ___ ___   ___ ___ ___ -
96   53   59   96   61   82

___ ___ ___ ___ ___ ___ ___ ___ ___
43   61   55   53   43   59   62   75   43

Name: _____ Date: _____

Riddle 56

What's worse than finding a worm in your apple?

Add or subtract.
Solve the riddle using your answers.

$$52 + 23$$

D

$$77 - 27$$

F

$$34 + 15$$

L

$$99 - 13$$

H

$$72 - 35$$

A

$$59 + 32$$

W

$$82 - 17$$

I

$$19 + 22$$

M

$$29 + 16$$

O

$$89 - 37$$

N

$$43 + 23$$

R

$$90 - 17$$

G

Solve the Riddle! Write the letter that goes with each number.

___ ___ ___ ___ ___ ___ ___
50   65   52   75   65   52   73

___ ___ ___ ___   ___   ___ ___ ___
86 37 49 50   37   91 45 66 41

Name: _____ Date: _____

Riddle 57

What do you call a whale that talks and talks and talks?

Add or subtract.
Solve the riddle using your answers.

64	55	43	66	85	46
+23	−31	+51	−24	−27	+46
___	___	___	___	___	___
L	N	B	T	E	O

92	48	46	98	46	80
−45	+33	+37	−59	+47	−64
___	___	___	___	___	___
U	S	H	A	M	R

Solve the Riddle!   Write the letter that goes with each number.

___ ___ ___ ___ ___ ___ ___ ___
39 94 87 47 94 94 58 16

___ ___ ___ ___ ___
93 92 47 42 83

Answer Key

page 5: **Riddle 1**
on a bunnymoon
A-4, B-6, C-9, D-11, M-13, N-15, O-18, R-20,
S-21, T-22, U-23, Y-24

page 6: **Riddle 2**
in the dark
A-31, E-28, H-34, N-36, T-43, S-42, D-30, F-29,
I-40, K-38, R-41, W-49

page 7: **Riddle 3**
ferry tales
A-55, C-56, G-53, I-57, R-71, T-68, B-59, F-51,
E-60, L-69, S-74, Y-72

page 8: **Riddle 4**
They don't know how to cook.
A-75, C-81, E-84, K-87, O-91, W-98, B-77,
D-86, H-79, N-89, T-96, Y-99

page 9: **Riddle 5**
a blab-oon
A-2, D-4, N-0, R-8, B-5, E-7, O-9, S-10, C-3,
L-1, P-6, Y-11

page 10: **Riddle 6**
punch
A-10, D-15, H-14, P-13, W-18, C-12, E-17, N-19,
S-20, U-11

page 11: **Riddle 7**
Open her refrigerator.
A-3, E-9, F-11, G-16, H-20, F-13, N-18, O-21, P-17,
I-14, R-19, T-10

page 12: **Riddle 8**
club sandwiches
C-11, D-21, A-32, E-41, H-31, I-43, L-27, N-51, S-18,
W-42, U-49, B-29

page 13: **Riddle 9**
to catch the bus
D-61, B-72, C-83, E-74, H-81, O-76, R-96, S-51,
T-93, U-54, A-94, Z-100

page 14: **Riddle 10**
chocolate chirp
A-8, C-6, H-9, S-11, R-4, O-5, L-3, E-10, P-1, T-2,
I-7, N-12

page 15: **Riddle 11**
in the North pool
E-2, B-4, I-5, L-3, N-6, O-9, P-1, H-10, T-0, R-7,
A-11, D-8

page 16: **Riddle 12**
cheese and thank you
A-9, C-10, D-11, E-7, K-4, N-12, O-2, H-8, S-3, T-5,
U-1, Y-6

page 17: **Riddle 13**
He tasted funny.
A-12, E-4, D-8, H-7, N-3, F-10, P-11, Y-6, U-5,
S-9, T-2, S-9

page 18: **Riddle 14**
a sand-witch
N-24, S-16, H-18, T-12, A-13, W-25, I-10, J-15,
F-11, R-14, D-17, C-19

page 19: **Riddle 15**
under the covers
E-18, O-15, T-10, V-9, N-17, D-13, S-11, R-19,
C-22, U-8, D-16, H-7

page 20: **Riddle 16**
He was too unhoppy.
A-16, H-22, E-18, N-23, O-25, T-14, Y-11, S-19, W-6,
U-20, P-24, R-9

page 21: **Riddle 17**
wet sneakers
A-60, B-50, E-30, K-40, R-20, S-90, A-60, T-80,
N-10, W-70, D-100, S-90

page 22: **Riddle 18**
The sooner it is out, the better!
T-50, U-30, O-10, H-20, R-60, N-90, I-0, B-80,
E-70, S-40, L-100, T-50

page 23: **Riddle 19**
after breakfast
F-40, L-80, O-20, E-0, A-50, K-70, T-100, L-80,
S-90, B-60, R-10, D-30

page 24: **Riddle 20**
He had hay fever.
A-8, D-10, E-16, F-20, H-28, R-32, S-36, O-42, T-40,
Y-46, W-48, V-50

page 25: **Riddle 21**
buttered pup-corn
B-34, D-40, P-24, N-44, U-22, R-28, O-16, A-32, T-18, E-6, C-20, S-10

page 26: **Riddle 22**
all of them
O-42, F-18, S-48, D-12, A-28, E-22, T-8, R-32, L-12, M-38, H-50, N-4

page 27: **Riddle 23**
the outside
E-25, N-45, T-55, R-75, O-95, H-70, I-65, S-30, F-40, U-50, D-100, B-90

page 28: **Riddle 24**
Have a mice day.
A-5, Y-25, E-35, C-55, M-75, D-60, V-40, N-10, H-20, E-30, T-85, I-50

page 29: **Riddle 25**
big bad wolves
G-35, W-20, N-40, D-90, B-25, O-100, L-5, A-75, S-15, I-45, V-30, E-95

page 30: **Riddle 26**
It waves.

$$③ + ⑦ + 4 = \frac{14}{W} \qquad 5 + ③ + ⑦ = \frac{15}{I}$$

$$⑤ + 1 + ⑤ = \frac{11}{R} \qquad 3 + ⑥ + ④ = \frac{13}{S}$$

$$⑥ + ④ + 9 = \frac{19}{V} \qquad ② + 7 + ⑧ = \frac{17}{E}$$

$$⑧ + ② + 10 = \frac{20}{A} \qquad ⑥ + 2 + ④ = \frac{12}{N}$$

$$⑤ + 8 + ⑤ = \frac{18}{T}$$

page 31: **Riddle 27**
Let's be pen pals.

$$④ + ⑥ + 40 = \frac{50}{T} \qquad 25 + ③ + ⑦ = \frac{35}{E}$$

$$30 + ⑤ + ⑤ = \frac{40}{A} \qquad 35 + ⑥ + ④ = \frac{45}{R}$$

$$20 + ⑦ + ③ = \frac{30}{L} \qquad ① + 5 + ⑨ = \frac{15}{S}$$

$$⑧ + ② + 10 = \frac{20}{P} \qquad ⑥ + 0 + ④ = \frac{10}{N}$$

$$⑤ + 15 + ⑤ = \frac{25}{B}$$

page 32: **Riddle 28**
to get to the other slide
A-12, D-9, E-7, G-8, H-13, I-24, L-70, O-50, T-80, N-38, S-17, R-15

page 33: **Riddle 29**
A bat can fly but a fly can't bat.
B-9, F-5, T-6, C-12, L-14, A-20, Y-60, N-50, R-90, U-48, E-17, O-15

page 34: **Riddle 30**
one lost penguin
B-125, E-188, N-150, L-277, O-289, S-302, T-317, U-426, G-444, I-252, S-490, P-407

page 35: **Riddle 31**
bronze-asaurus
B-502, Z-700, U-550, M-688, R-829, E-718, S-860, D-926, O-745, N-826, A-990, T-907

page 36: **Riddle 32**
potato ships
T-36, E-25, N-81, S-60, O-77, H-48, U-19, A-53, I-29, P-12

page 37: **Riddle 33**
am-fib-ians
F-30, S-56, E-35, R-28, N-91, I-63, M-66, B-40, A-87, P-72

page 38: **Riddle 34**
water
A-125, E-206, W-634, T-519, C-922, N-390, D-411, R-817

page 39: **Riddle 35**
Sep-timmmber!
B-6, D-15, R-24, E-33, T-39, M-51, O-63, V-75, U-87, I-96, S-108, P-120

page 40: **Riddle 36**
a yardstick
A-8, N-24, D-40, C-56, K-64, R-80, O-96, S-112, I-132, Y-148, T-164, M-180

page 41: **Riddle 37**
a hippo-spotty-mus
S-10, I-25, Y-40, O-55, U-60, R-70, A-85, E-100, P-120, T-135, M-150, H-165

page 42: **Riddle 38**
tulips
E-102, T-108, A-114, I-120, S-126, N-135, U-144, R-153, L-180, D-195, F-210, P-225

page 43: **Riddle 39**
a lighthouse
T-162, U-171, E-180, L-189, H-200, A-212, G-224,
R-236, N-240, O-255, I-270, S-290

page 44: **Riddle 40**
'Tis the season to be jelly!
S-28, H-34, O-16, A-49, T-35, N-27, B-48, J-46,
Y-26, I-38, E-42, L-23

page 45: **Riddle 41**
in a dictionary
T-63, D-86, R-91, A-79, E-66, I-98, O-75, Y-94,
N-72, H-57, C-82, F-88

page 46: **Riddle 42**
She looks at her witch watch.
S-66, A-89, K-78, O-49, L-36, H-68, W-47, R-85,
C-42, E-54, T-92, I-98

page 47: **Riddle 43**
Be yourself.
Y-37, B-33, O-18, F-5, N-24, L-30, D-43, U-11,
T-14, E-25, R-2, S-28

page 48: **Riddle 44**
a pajama-saurus Rex
J-23, T-44, A-81, R-35, W-42, M-63, E-32, N-61,
P-84, X-50, S-70, U-73

page 49: **Riddle 45**
cow-operation
A-47, C-36, D-26, E-31, G-38, T-14, I-45, N-13,
O-25, P-32, R-37, W-44

page 50: **Riddle 46**
a chim-pansy
A-56, P-17, T-92, S-18, C-46, G-9, H-83, I-23,
K-74, M-28, N-51, Y-49

page 51: **Riddle 47**
because bananas peel
E-21, P-22, A-20, L-27, B-25, N-24, T-30, U-23, S-28,
C-26, D-30, A-20

page 52: **Riddle 48**
mice cream cones
I-32, R-46, D-35, E-42, O-47, B-31, M-44, A-40,
C-37, S-45, F-50, N-48

page 53: **Riddle 49**
She takes it easel.
A-73, S-66, I-85, R-62, K-55, P-91, W-76, T-57,
L-88, H-70, E-61, N-98

page 54: **Riddle 50**
Her teeth were not loose.
R-13, E-16, L-6, W-9, N-18, T-7, P-25, D-15, S-17,
Y-14, O-3, H-19

page 55: **Riddle 51**
tuba two
B-17, N-6, S-18, U-15, M-21, T-19, E-23, A-7, D-9,
W-28, O-16, H-26

page 56: **Riddle 52**
a cow going backwards
W-14, R-79, A-18, N-75, S-61, C-38, I-33, K-27,
G-49, D-29, B-58, O-67

page 57: **Riddle 53**
Now glow to sleep.
G-14, R-25, L-9, N-24, O-22, T-17, P-23, I-35, S-12,
A-20, W-7, E-21

page 58: **Riddle 54**
They are too big to iron.
E-8, O-28, B-19, Y-9, G-21, T-5, A-18, S-17, H-7,
I-39, N-15, R-14

page 59: **Riddle 55**
her hop-tometrist
R-59, O-61, H-96, I-62, E-53, A-92, M-55, D-80,
S-75, P-82, N-72, T-43

page 60: **Riddle 56**
finding half a worm
D-75, F-50, L-49, H-86, A-37, W-91, I-65, M-41,
O-45, N-52, R-66, G-73

page 61: **Riddle 57**
a blubber mouth
L-87, N-24, B-94, T-42, E-58, O-92, U-47, S-81,
H-83, A-39, M-93, R-16